No Fear, Just God
When Fear Met My God Given Destiny

My Story

No Fear, Just God!

Dedications

I dedicate this book to two special people;

To my grandmother, Mabril Tee Donahue, I dedicate this book to you because your strength and your faith in God have taught me so much in life. I love that no matter what you have endured, you still gave God glory and credit for keeping you. You are the perfect example of the Proverbs 31[1] woman. Tee Bird, I love you with all of my heart and I am so grateful that you are an example in my life.

And to my Aunt Gloria, who stood in the gap for all of her nieces and nephews and helped raise us. You inspired me to always do my best. When you left in 2007, it was left a major impact on my life but I never ever forgot what you have taught me and showed me. I have accomplished so much since you have been gone and I wish that

---

[1] Proverbs 31 refers to the "Virtuous Woman" as mentioned in Proverbs 31:10 of the King James Version
Who can find a virtuous woman? For her price is far above rubies.

3

you were here physically to share it all, but I know you are with me every day and step of the way.

This is for YOU! .... With love, Sista

Contents

Introduction

I appear to have it all together on the outside. However,

the truth of the matter is, at some point, fear had eaten away at

me until it had become unbearable. A lot of it was self-inflected.

I cannot even blame the devil on this one. Well, I do not want to

blame it on the devil because he will not get credit for how my

journey started or how it will end.

Ecclesiastes 3:1-8[2] says: *To every thing there is a season, and a time*

to every purpose under the heaven:² A time to be born, and a time to die; a

time to plant, and a time to pluck up that which is planted;³ A time to kill, and

a time to heal; a time to break down, and a time to build up;⁴ A time to weep,

and a time to laugh; a time to mourn, and a time to dance;⁵ A time to cast

away stones, and a time to gather stones together; a time to embrace, and a

time to refrain from embracing;⁶ A time to get, and a time to lose; a time to

keep, and a time to cast away;⁷ A time to rend, and a time to sew; a time to

---

[2] Ecclesiastes 3:1-8 King James Version

keep silence, and a time to speak;[8] A time to love, and a time to hate; a time of war, and a time of peace.

When I read this scripture, it does not miss anything that I have come across in life. I have always had the option to make Godly choices but sometimes it is hard to see and think clearly with fear involved. This journey taught me a lot. It helped me to grow spiritually, emotionally and physically.

Enjoy my story!

No Fear, Just God!

No Fear

"For God hath not given us the Spirit of Fear,

but of power, and of love,

and of a sound mind."

II Timothy 1:7[3]

Fear is unpleasant. It is an emotion induced by a threat perceived by living entities. This emotion causes a change in the brain and organ functions and ultimately a change in behavior. Some behavioral examples include but are not limited to running away, hiding or freezing. Fear has a physical effect on our body, and our mind.

What causes fear? Fear is expressed at increasing levels as worry, anxiety, dread, terror and panic. These levels are

---

[3] II Timothy 1:7 King James Version

determined by the imminence of danger. Worry and anxiety are triggered by the anticipation of being harmed in the future. Dread, terror and panic are emotions that concern or display themselves in the immediate present. At the highest levels, terror and panic overwhelm people, causing them to make irrational choices. While terror is an apprehension of impending danger, horror is a sickening and painful experience. Horror is the emotion that lays the foundation for the amygdalae to sense the backgrounds of painful events. The amygdalae remembers the image, sound, words and situations which accompanied the horror of injury, ridicule, social rejection, loss of loved ones, or career failure. Subsequently, the detection of any related signals trigger fear. Often without the person knowing the cause of one's fear.

We find that fear has a chain of reactions. It goes from one source to the next and eventually triggers the emotion in our body. Have you wondered how to recognize fear? Here are some points. On receiving fear signals from the amygdalae, the hypothalamus, acts reflexively to control the reproductive, vegetative, endocrine, hormonal, visceral and autonomic functions of the body. Breathing, digesting, blood circulation, brain activity and body fluid flows are instantly affected. The signals from the amygdale dilate pupils and increase brain wave frequency. They make hairs stand on end. They reduce saliva, drying the mouth. They cause sweating and a decrease in skin resistance. They decrease peripheral blood flow and cause hands to become cold. The signals speed breathing and dilate bronchial tubes to allow more air to the lungs. They tighten stomach muscles, slow digestion and close down the excretory system. They increase acids in the stomach, causing diarrhea.

The signals travel to the adrenal gland, which produces cortisol, causing an increase in glucose production to provide additional fuel for the muscles and brain to deal with the potential stress. The signals increase blood pressure, release

sugar into the blood and increase the tendency for blood

clotting. The signals increase red blood cells. They tense

postural muscles to allow greater blood flow. They slow the

working of the immune system. The amygdalae trigger a chain

of biological events and engulf the mind in the fear emotion,

even before the conscious mind can assess the situation. In the

modern world, such persistent fear signals are not set off by real

physical danger. They are triggered by an instinctive brain,

which tries to overcome social and career issues by foolishly

preparing the body to freeze, flee or defend itself. By

understanding the physiological response our bodies have to

fear, it can be understood just how crippling fear is to fulfilling

God's ordained purpose for our lives.

We, those of us living a Christian lifestyle, have allowed

fear to separate and or rob us of the things God wants to give us.

Those things lost are ours! They belonged to us. But, somehow, because of fear, we talked ourselves right out of our blessings; blessings God made especially for our enjoyment.

Fear has a negative impact in our everyday life. Fear of not being qualified has kept many of us from job elevations. Past hurts and disappointment of failed relationships have kept us from having successful marriages because we fear being hurt again.

"No Fear, Just God" was a message given to me during a time in my life when the enemy was trying to "punk"[4] my spirit. The enemy decided to challenge my foundation that was and is built on the Word of God. Throughout this book, I will be transparent and share many moments of fear I have faced in my life. By my transparency, it is hoped that my experiences will help bring hope to you the reader that you can live without fear. Living without fear will positively change your life.

---

[4] Punk in this tense of the word refers to being made a coward, lacking courage.

Fear has no respect of your Christian background or your church membership. Some of the greatest people in the world will attest to having a fearful moment at some point in their life that served to drive them away from the assignment God had planned for them. Giving into fear is not necessarily a negative character trait. Sometimes we are simply caught off guard and lose focus of the task at hand.

The enemy set traps for me; traps to cause me to fail. He sets traps that I would be unsuccessful in all that I do such as operating in the flesh and not in the spirit, making moves without consulting God, being put in a worse position that I was when I started, but God!

One of my favorite scriptures is Zechariah 4:10[5] *"For who hath despised the day of small things? For these seven shall rejoice, and shall see the plummet in the land of Zerubbabel; these are the eyes of Jehovah, which run to and fro through the*

---

[5] Zechariah 4:10 King James Version

whole earth. I came in this world to some a small thing but the greatness on the inside was huge, and it was mighty."

Prayer against Fear

Father God,

I come thankful for Your power and thankful for the victory over fear. Believing that without You, oh God, things will never and can never change. God, I pray for the person who is reading this book and has the desire to overcome this thing called 'fear', which has been the enemy's biggest trap for believers. I pray that as we enter into the chapters of this book, that my story will help deliver and set my brothers and sisters free. I pray, God, through this book that someone will come to know You better and grow in their relationship with You. God, I pray that You will remove the spirit of fear in every area of their lives so they can live a life that is pleasing unto you. God, give us patience to wait while you work. Give us the desire to want more of You, oh God. As your Word declares, we were not given the spirit of fear[6], so we rebuke fear, in the name of Jesus.

The Spirit of fear is released! Give us grace and favor!

In Jesus' name, I pray. Amen!

---

[6] II Timothy 1:7 King James Version refer to the top of page 5 for full scripture text.

No Fear, Just God!

Birthed into the Fear of Living

"For I know the plans for you,

declares the Lord.

Plans to prosper you and not be harm you,

Plans to give you hope and a future."

Jeremiah 29:11 [7]

I was born December 13, 1979 to my wonderful parents, Pastor Norman and Diane Donahue. The birth of a child, for the most part, is a joyous occasion. However, who would have thought, on this day, I would have my first experience with fear? For obvious reasons I was neither aware nor equipped to handle it. For the first 24 hours of my life, the doctors FEARED I would not make it. I was born prematurely, weighing four

---

[7] Jeremiah 29:11 King James Version

pounds and nine ounces with a list of medical problems. Since I was so small and born with pneumonia and a digestive illness, everyone FEARED the worst for me, but God! Thankfully, God already predestined my days and His design for me was already laid out.

It was now up to God, to whom my family entrusted my life, to confirm the plan that He had for my life.

After receiving the doctor's report, my parents, instead of being consumed with the FEAR of the unknown, decided to call the One that was known for being FEARLESS. There were prayer warriors called in to pray on my behalf during this critical time. Many family members and friends actively prayed for me and were present for my parents. They prayed FEAR away and life coupled with favor into me, so that I may live to tell the story; when doctors said NO God has the power to say YES. He will turn things completely around.

In know that my life was planned for me, after my initial encounter with fear, I would soon face it again.

After leaving the hospital, I began to struggle with health issues that alleviated over time. I suffered with the lasting effects of asthma. Even with that hurdle, I was blessed with the gift to sing. Between the ages of five and six, I developed a love for music that has never interrupted by any breathing problems.

This encounter with God set me on a path that always made me stand out. I remember how my father testified about my story and how he thanked God for healing me. I also recall Pastor Napoleon Wordlaw, Jr. as he called me, "God's Miracle Baby". He still calls me this today.

I spent the last week of my grandfather's life with him. One of those days spent with him fell on my 27th birthday. He encouraged me to be myself, and went on to share with me that God saved me for a purpose. He said I was different and unique and would always be set apart from the rest. I could not agree with him more because it has been confirmed in my life today. While there is more work to accomplish, my beginning set me up for my today and my tomorrows.

Prayers for Preemies

Gracious God,

Creator of the most precious, tiny, babies. God, I come standing in position seeking Your covering for every premature infant born. I pray, God, that You will give them healing in every area of their little bodies. I pray, God, that Your creative power will develop whatever is physically missing. I ask that You will give normal, healthy, stable lives and that every chance of a good living will be made available to them. We pray God that they grow up to be God-fearing children and adults. I pray they will look and marvel at what You have done for them. God, I also stand in pray for the parents who have to witness their babies struggle. I pray for every doctor and nurse assigned to their care. Give them the tools and resources to handle this special gift with care. Watch over and guide them. In Jesus' name, I pray.

Amen.

No Fear, Just God!

Bullied into the Fear of Growing Up

"I can do all things through Christ

that strengthens me."

Philippians 4:13[8]

After all of the praying, speaking loving life, and pulling through against all odds, I made it! Then the unthinkable happened.

After I conquered death as an infant, in my early childhood, I encountered fear yet again. I enjoyed going to school until the fourth grade. I was bullied for the remainder of my elementary school years. Do not get me wrong, I knew how to fight and defend myself. I was the last born of four children. I have a sister, Tavia, and two brothers, Norman, Jr. and Kevin.

---

[8] Philippians 4:13 New King James Version

Growing up in the house with them, reflecting back, I had no worries. Even though I was the baby, I did not enjoy this role. I often wanted to be as big as my siblings and do what they did. I had a hard time accepting the fact that I was just the baby. My sister and I have a large gap between us, so when I got of age, she was away at college. Her being in college left me with the boys; they protected and took good care of their little sister.

I knew how to fight and those lessons would pay off in elementary school. For some reason, outside of my home, fear took control of me. I cried to get out of going to school. I did not enjoy learning. School felt like the scariest place ever due to the bullying. No matter what I did to maintain good grades, they suffered due to the stressful environment.

It is true that wounded people wound others. While in the seventh grade, I was no longer bullied because I was now the bully. Even though I knew right from wrong, I chose to do wrong. I bullied others to keep the pressure off me. Unbeknownst to me, because of this period of my life, Wounded Women Ministry was born. I was wounded, so I wounded others. I hurt people with my words, expressions and definitely my attitude.

When elementary school ended, I thought the fear would end as well. It did not. It simply changed its form. Even though I bullied as a defense mechanism, after being bullied, it did not assuage the hurt or heal the unforgiveness built up after I had endured years of mistreatment.

Entering high school made no difference. While I knew I had a new start in a different school, my past fears reestablished themselves in this setting. The dark cloud of longing for acceptance and love followed me until my sophomore year at Proviso East High School.

It was then I met LeAundre Hill, who changed my entire outlook on life. LeAundre gave me a sense of hope to live, to forgive, and to trust again. To some, LeAundre was the wrong fit for me, and many tried their best to keep us apart with lies, rumors and nasty comments. We heard, "He's too old for you! He has a child! He has an independent life going on!" If I had as many babies as people claimed we had, we would not be able to keep count!

The saddest part of this situation was the behavior of some church people. It became so overwhelming! It taught us, if nothing else, to pray together and stick it out. We are so glad we listened to God and made the choice to stay together. Nineteen years later, we are still friends. He was a true Godsend and I fell hard! When he came into my life things changed for the better and have been amazing since, well, almost.

Even though I was bullied, I want to make it clear that I had a wonderful childhood. I was full of life and energy. Some of my best days were spent on 10th and Harvard. The summers spent here made getting older so grand!

My parents believed that the kids belong in the house when the streetlights came on but that did not stop us from having fun. We ran up and down that block everyday as if it was the best thing ever.

Take a trip with me down memory lane: basketball at the Haywood's or Bosley's home, piggy softball in the street, the girl clubs we created. Those were the days! We laughed, we cried, and we got each other through many rough patches. Tenth Avenue was a block that believed in helping one another.

My family was also known for hosting gatherings at our house. The Stanley and Moore family, along with Aunt Claudia, Gloria, and many more would join us for Pizza Night on Friday.

We ordered Garbage Can Pizza[9], drank Coke®[10] and Orange

soda. On nights before the holiday, we stayed up to shave

carrots, slice onions, and peel eggs. We did whatever we could

to help Sweetie Ma cook for the big family dinners. My poor

dad always reminded me of *The Cosby Show*[11] episode when Dr.

Huxtable ran in and out the house, back and forth to the store in

the rain. That was my dad and brother's job.

Saturday nights were magically special. They were

nights for my bonding time with my mom and sister. When I

came in the house from playing outside, I would open the door

and hear Father Hayes' broadcast blasted. I knew then that it

was time to get my hair shampooed, blow dried, and curled.

The kitchen filled with smoke from Blue Magic®[12] oil sizzling

on the pressing comb. My mom made her own conditioner for

---

[9] Garbage can pizza is a pizza with every topping imaginable on it.

[10] Coke® is registered and trademarked by Coca-Cola Company

[11] The Cosby Show originally aired on NBC from 1984-1992 Produced by Carsey-Werner Productions and Bill Cosby

[12] Blue Magic® is registered and trademarked by J. Strickland & Co. Cosmetics

our hair using eggs and mayonnaise. The smell alone was gag worthy, yuck! She just knew it was the best thing since sliced bread.

Family is important to me. Anyone that knows me would agree that I would do anything for them, even to the point of sacrificing myself. I just love, love, love my people. Being around family is the only time fear could not rob me of happiness and feeling complete. My family was my safety net. I felt protected and loved unconditionally. No matter what, I knew they had my back and I theirs.

Fear however lurked on Fifth and Keeler on the Westside of Chicago. When visiting my grandparents' home there was a family that lived on my grandparents' block that scared me. They bullied every child on the block! I was so afraid of them that being on the street during playtime caused anxiety. When we pulled up to my grandparents' home, I prayed that the family of torturers moved far away. To my dismay, they would be outside and I trembled in fright.

One visit, my grandmother had enough! She was tired of the fear and tears. As usual, they chased us back to my grandparents' house as we screamed, but this time was different. My grandmother met us at the door, asked us what happened and replied, "You mean to tell me, it's four of you and one of him, and he has all of you running in fear of *him?*" I tried to explain and said, "But Grandma, it may just be one, but he also has a dog chain that he hit one of us with!" She looked at us and said, "It's more of you that it is of him, now get back out there and don't let nobody run you back in this house or you will have to deal with me!" We marched outside with no fear of that family. We learned something in that moment, there was something bigger than fear, and it was grandma! We never were picked on by that family again. This same lesson can be applied spiritually. Just as my grandmother was more threatening than the fear of the family on the block, so is God. God is greater than fear. We can be still and know that God is God. [13] Deuteronomy 20:1 states: *When thou goest out to battle against thine enemies, and seest horses, and chariots, and a people more than thou, be not afraid of them, for the LORD thy God is with thee, which brought thee up out of the land of Egypt.* [14]

---

[13] Psalm 46:10 King James Version *Be still, and know that I am God: I will be exalted among the heathen; I will be exalted in the earth.*
[14] Deuteronomy 20:1 King James Version

Prayer against the Spirit of Bullying

Father God,

I come to You praying that the spirit of bullying will cease. I pray God that you will uproot it and destroy it in the name of Jesus. God, I pray for the detrimental impact it has made on so many children and adults the residue of unforgiveness, hurt, and shame that stained their hearts. God, we pray for restoration for every child or teen who once contemplated suicide because of how they were mistreated by their peers in the name of Jesus. God, I pray that every negative seed that has been planted in the minds of the precious child that has to face a bully daily will not take root but will be destroyed in the mighty name of Jesus.

I pray for a special covering and protection in agreement with your Word that reminds us when the enemy comes in like flood that you will raise up a standard against it. [15] Oh God, I pray that You will touch the mind of the one that is doing the bullying; that You will change their mindset and their way of reacting to their own hurt. I pray for peace, Father, in their mind and love in their hearts so they can live without hurting others. God hear my plea. In Jesus' name, I pray. Amen!

---

[15] Isaiah 59:19 King James Version *So shall they fear the name of the LORD from the west, and his glory from the rising of the sun. When the enemy shall come in like a flood, the Spirit of the LORD shall lift up a standard against him.*

Fear of Life and Death

"The thief cometh not, but to steal, and to kill, and to destroy;

I am come that they might have life and they

might have it more abundantly."

John 10:19[16]

In 1998, I experienced true fear of life and death. As a follower of Christ, I know the Bible says, in Job 14:1 [17] *"Man that is born of a woman is of few days and full of trouble."* As a P.K,[18] I have had my share of supporting and serving those who lost loved ones. However, 1998 would be the year my family was shaken.

---

[16] John 10:19 King James Version
[17] Job 14:1 King James Version
[18] Preacher's/Pastor's Kid

Nineteen hundred and ninety-eight was my senior year in high school. Mr. Hill and I were doing well and my mind was free of some issues. One day, my father picked up my friend and me from school as was his custom. When we got in the car, he was unusually quiet. The silence was awkward. He broke his silence with news that my grandmother, Mrs. Janie Bostic, had a massive stroke and passed away. The fear that I fought against for so long crept back up in record time. I dreaded the effect of this news would damage and hurt my mother and her siblings to the core. I feared death! Because of death, life as we knew it was shaken and turned upside down. What I feared was correct. My grandmother was an awesome woman. She helped raise some of my cousins as her own children. The devastation of losing the rock of the family caused many foundations to be unsettled.

A short time later, my grandfather, Mr. Leroy Bostic returned from a ride to the doctor's office. After thanking my aunt for caring for him and my grandmother, he got out of the car and collapsed. A few steps away from his front door he died from a heart attack. We supported and loved my mom through the loss of both parents within an 18-month timespan. My grandparents lived in Tennessee so we did not see them often; however, they played big roles in our lives. Our down south summers were a blast. 'BoBo' would take us out when he went to work and we rode in the back of his red pickup truck, up hills and down hills. Some days he sold fish to the locals. We went down to the river where men fished and my grandfather picked up two tubs of fish and went and sold them. He also owned a swing in the 'hole' [19] and he took us there to swing and ride around and around to attract other kids to come over and buy tickets to ride. As long as I can remember, my grandfather always had multiple jobs and was a great provider for his family.

---

[19] The local park in the area of Tennessee.

It must be said that I truly am not fit for corporate America simply because I am 'Trump' Bostic's granddaughter. In the time we, my immediate family and I, spent with him, he showed us how to make a living and to be self-sufficient. He was adamant about not letting emotions interfere with his business.

I know that someday we all have to leave this Earth. No one will last an eternity in mortal flesh. Fear of life and death can be a bit overwhelming. It is a concept that is hard to understand. It is hard to obtain peace knowing the Lord numbers our days.

In 2006, we found ourselves providing the same comfort for my father that we did for my mother. My paternal grandfather, Deacon Jessie Donahue, a great man, departed this life two days after my 27th birthday. He passed away just as I accepted the fact that all of us leave this Earth someday. It was one of the hardest moments of my life and changed me forever.

His death challenged me spiritually and emotionally. After my grandfather died, fear of living was acutely real. We prayed to God to heal my grandfather, and he seemed to get better. The very day he passed away, my husband and I supported our friend who lost her husband to cancer. The church where our friend's funeral was held was down the street from my grandfather's home. My husband and I checked on my grandfather before we went to the funeral. He laughed, was in great spirits. Nothing seemed unusual. He had an appointment for his second round of dialysis and told us he did not want to do it. As we left, I told him he had to do what the doctor ordered to get better. Little did I know, in that moment, I was speaking to the spirit within him and not actually to the physical being. For it was later that evening, after he returned from dialysis, he passed away.

In my mind, I could not make the fact that he died mesh with the promise God made to heal him. I later realized that I feared we would miss him and would struggle without my

grandfather around. I also feared my grandmother, who was

very close her spouse, my grandfather, would not be able to get

through life without her helpmate. This caused me to be

depressed and angry with God. Without realizing it, every day, I

became more and more detached from God.

Due to the unexpected death, I operated on a few hours

of sleep daily. I became dependent on medicine to help me sleep

at night. On the nights when Benadryl®[20] did not help, I resorted

to 'nightcaps'.[21] Since I was not a drinker, a cap of wine was

pretty much all I needed to fall asleep. The persistent lack of

sleep eventually led me to use of Norco®[22], Flexeril®[23], and

Tylenol 3®[24]

---

[20] Benadryl®- Over the counter medicine by Johnson & Johnson and McNeil Consumer Healthcare.

[21] Night caps- an alcoholic beverage consumed before sleeping at night

[22] Norco®- Trade brand name of Hydrocodone/paracetamol- a pain reliever with common side effect of drowsiness

[23] Flexeril®- Trade brand name of Cyclobenzaprine- a muscle relaxant with common side effect of drowsiness

[24] Tylenol with Codeine #3®- Trade brand name of Acetaminophen and Codeine- a pain reliever with a common side effect of sleepiness

I did not realize it then but I had become addicted and dependent upon these prescription drugs to get to sleep at night, instead of depending on God. I would stay up all night long. During this time, I wanted nothing to do with God. I felt he took the man that smiled and lit up any room away prematurely. He laughed and I forgot about every care of the world. Most importantly, he was a man that faithfully served God. He made Christianity look easy and necessary to have a good life.

When God called him home, a man that served God endlessly; it exposed my true level of faith. I was confused. From the moment my husband said my grandfather passed away, it felt like my mind could not rest. Everything about me changed from my demeanor, attitude, even my will to live. I was so far out of my mind. I was known to sing and lead worship, I worshipped God with all my heart, but honestly, during this time there was no desire to do that. I remained this way for a year or more. I missed my mentor; he was one of the greatest men in my life. Instead of turning to God that my grandfather taught me about and instilled in me, the fear of living without my grandfather caused me to turn to myself. I tried to figure things out on my own. Fear of living can potentially lead to destruction and or death if not remedied.

Thank God for my cousin, LaTosha Holden! She recognized the changes and got help for me. It is amazing how I was able to function and move through life for years without the acceptance of how fear had me on a downward spiral. After I received counsel, I realized there was no need to have fear; I needed God, just God. His will for everyone's life is already established. Life and death are by his power and might. We have no say in how God handles His business.[25] We have to trust Him and that He will make sure we are covered during the process.

---

[25] Proverbs 19:21 New International Version *Many are the plans in a person's heart, but it is the LORD'S purpose that prevails.*

What some people are afraid of is death. That should never be the case if you have a relationship with God. The fear of death is for the unbeliever because their eternity is unknown. But when a believer dies in Christ, there is no fear because the believer will rest in heaven for an eternity. God prepared a place for those that believe, a place where peace and joy last forever. In this, we find hope; whatever we have to run from on Earth, we will get rest from in Glory.

When my grandparents and others departed, it always saddened me. I was especially saddened when my Aunt Gloria passed away five months after my paternal grandfather. My Aunt Gloria was the Bostic family's glue. She held it all and everyone together. She was selfless, whatever she had, she gave out. Aunt Gloria was an RN[26] at Hines Veteran's Administration Hospital and Baptist Memorial Hospital in Memphis TN. She was the best to have on staff and our family called her with

---

[26]Registered Nurse

symptoms often. She told us our ailment and what to tell the doctors.

Just when I was convinced my life was cursed and ruined, God showed me His hand. Yes, death stings and causes one to be unsure, but God is a part of it all and He had a plan. Sometimes we will question God, but know that even in death, He is still an awesome and amazing God with a purpose and plan for our lives.

I have found hope in the following:

II Corinthians 5[27]

[1] For we know that if our earthly house of this tabernacle were dissolved, we have a building of God, an house not made with hands, eternal in the heavens.

[2] For in this we groan, earnestly desiring to be clothed upon with our house which is from heaven:

[3] If so be that being clothed we shall not be found naked.

[4] For we that are in this tabernacle do groan, being burdened: not for that we would be unclothed, but clothed upon, that mortality might be swallowed up of life.

[5] Now he that hath wrought us for the selfsame thing is God, who also hath given unto us the earnest of the Spirit.

[6] Therefore we are always confident, knowing that, whilst we are at home in the body, we are absent from the Lord:

[7] (For we walk by faith, not by sight:)

[8] We are confident, I say, and willing rather to be absent from the body, and to be present with the Lord.

[9] Wherefore we labour, that, whether present or absent, we may be accepted of him.

[10] For we must all appear before the judgment seat of Christ; that every one may receive the things done in his body, according to that he hath done, whether it be good or bad.

---

[27] II Corinthians 5 King James Version

[11] *Knowing therefore the terror of the Lord, we persuade men; but we are made manifest unto God; and I trust also are made manifest in your consciences.*

[12] *For we commend not ourselves again unto you, but give you occasion to glory on our behalf, that ye may have somewhat to answer them which glory in appearance, and not in heart.*

[13] *For whether we be beside ourselves, it is to God: or whether we be sober, it is for your cause.*

[14] *For the love of Christ constraineth us; because we thus judge, that if one died for all, then were all dead:*

[15] *And that he died for all, that they which live should not henceforth live unto themselves, but unto him which died for them, and rose again.*

[16] *Wherefore henceforth know we no man after the flesh: yea, though we have known Christ after the flesh, yet now henceforth know we him no more.*

[17] *Therefore if any man be in Christ, he is a new creature: old things are passed away; behold, all things are become new.*

[18] *And all things are of God, who hath reconciled us to himself by Jesus Christ, and hath given to us the ministry of reconciliation;*

[19] *To wit, that God was in Christ, reconciling the world unto himself, not imputing their trespasses unto them; and hath committed unto us the word of reconciliation.*

[20] *Now then we are ambassadors for Christ, as though God did beseech you by us: we pray you in Christ's stead, be ye reconciled to God.*

[21] *For he hath made him to be sin for us, who knew no sin; that we might be made the righteousness of God in him.*

Broken

Dear God,

I come praying for the broken, who have encountered the sting of the death of a loved one; the one, of God that has felt the lasting impact of Your will; the one, Master, who is having a hard time understanding Your doing. I pray for them today that even when we cannot see or understand what You are doing, that we have enough faith to trust what You are doing. Even, Father, when we do not know what You are doing we can find peace in knowing that it is YOUR doing. This prayer is for the broken and the bereaved, who have to make life adjustments without the everyday presence of their family or friend. God, we decree and declare that the empty void be filled, in the name of Jesus. That the spirit of depression be dismissed, in the name of Jesus. Those addictions formed as the result of coping mechanisms are done away with, in the precious name of Jesus. God I speak peace right now. Where there is sorrow, we speak joy. God please let them find rest in You. Please remind them that everything will be all right. Thank you for the 'angels' You have given us and the time they spent with us on this Earth, realizing that they belong to You.

We will be forever grateful. In Jesus Name! Amen!

Accepting It Is No Fear, Just God

"The Lord is my shepherd; I shall not want.

He maketh me to lie down in green pastures:

he leadeth me beside the still waters.

He restoreth my soul: he leadeth me in the paths of

righteousness for his name's sake.

Yea, though I walk through the valley of the shadow of death,

I will fear no evil: for thou art with me;

thy rod and thy staff they comfort me.

Thou preparest a table before me in the presence of mine enemies:

thou anointest my head with oil; my cup runneth over.

Surely goodness and mercy shall follow me all the days of my life:

and I will dwell in the house of the Lord for ever."

Psalm 23[28]

I have endured a lot in my 34 years of life. I found ways

to live and coexist with fear as a constant companion. Even

---

[28] Psalm 23 King James Version

though I knew God had greater for me, it still took years to realize the greatness inside of me. After allowing fear to run me away from my calling for five years, I preached my trial sermon on October 7, 2007. I feared because I grew up under a very strict traditional Baptist doctrine. As long as I could remember, women were not allowed to preach. This is actually taught in Baptist seminary schools. Due to my fear of being rejected, I ran as long as I could. That was until God increased my life with greater demands.

When I preached or taught, my ministry had developed and I was in line to minister to the lost and broken. I had nothing to fear. God called me and would always be with me. My gender did not matter; He set me apart to speak His Word. With that challenge came great responsibility. I studied, prepared, and walked away. When I accepted God's call, it caused me to step away from many people who just did not line up in that season for my life. I also realized that it was not fear. It was all God.

I have not stopped since I preached my initial sermon. I do not give fear an opportunity to slow me down or enter my mind. My goal is pleasing God and saving those that have been wounded. During my years of ministry, God continued to use me, especially with young adult women. In April 2011, I birthed my very own ministry, Wounded Women Ministry, WWM. The mission of WWM is to aid, uplift, and encourage women to strive and be the best that God had intended them to be. WWM has been a blessing to so many over the Chicagoland area and many other city and states. I knew the possibility that there were women out there that was just like me, and allowed fear to keep them from asking for help. So I decided after all I had been through and God bringing me out of it, that this was my opportunity to help someone else. It does not matter the race or religion, God sent me to go minister to the wounded.

You will be amazed at what you can accomplish when you remove fear and allow God to talk full charge of your life. I knew the Word of God but that does not mean I always applied it to my life. Allowing fear to rule is the quickest way to lose your grip on life. It will begin to slip out of your fingers.

Fear takes control when I lose focus. Now that is just for me, it is not the case for everyone. No matter what, today is the day we can determine to live like God is in full control. Nothing else matters.

Know that everyone has a ministry and God has set us all apart for a purpose. The key to fulfilling your purpose is removing whatever is hindering you from achieving it. God loves to see us in His will. He loves His children to follow His commands. Nothing makes a parent more proud than to see your children following the sound advice you have been given advice geared towards making life so much easier. Also, to have the pleasure to see it all unfold. God loves to see His children prosper, and be well. Love the life He has given us. We were designed to give Him glory and accept His will for our lives.

Prayer Requesting Forgiveness

Dear God,

It is our desire to do thy holy, diving will. We must first apologize to you, Father, for allowing emotions and fear to stand in the way of us hearing Your voice. Please forgive us for not listening to Your direction and being afraid when You told us to move. God, it was never our intent to put anything before You and lose focus of our assignment. We thank You for never letting go of our hands, Master, and continuing to hold unto us. Even when we did not deserve it God, You were still a father to us. Thank You for Your word that ensures that we do not have to worry about anything; that You will always be there for us. We do not have to fear because You have rule over everything. God, we surrender our will for Yours, we give ourselves totally today. God, You can trust us with the assignment you have prepared for us. Keep us, Dear God, is our prayer. In Jesus Name! Amen!

The Fear of Becoming a Wife and Mother

"For this cause shall a man leave his father and mother,

and shall be joined unto his wife, and they two shall be

one flesh. This is a great mystery: but I speak concerning

Christ and the church. Nevertheless, let every one of you

in particular so love his wife even as himself; and the

wife see that she reverence her husband."

Ephesians 5:31-33[29]

I met my husband in 1995 and I had no idea that he was

going to be my husband... wait... Yes, I knew it from the

beginning. So why did I have fear of being a wife? I was so

young and the mandate of being a successful wife was far

removed from me.

---

[29] Ephesians 5:31-33 New International Version

We were great friends, he was easy to talk to, but let us face it, we were both spoiled brats! At that age, all we knew were our parents and grandparents. We had no manual on how to be a husband or a wife. I wanted him, all of him with no interruptions and he wanted all of me with no one in between us. At first it was impossible because we were the go to people and our families depended on us for everything. The fear was present when the vows were said, and now it is time for two families to blend. The stories of in-law madness were overwhelming especially for a bride to be. LeAundre and my love was evident that we were not going anywhere. So proud to say our families came together well, we even worshipped together at my father's church[30] for some years. God blessed the Donahue's and the Hill's to be a big family.

---

[30] Three Crosses of Calvary Missionary Baptist Church · 4445 West Madison St. Chicago, IL, 60624

"Lo children are an heritage of the LORD; and the fruit of the womb is his award." Psalm 127:4[31]

I knew that I was destined to be a mother. Growing up I have always loved babies, children and they loved me. Whether it was in church, baby-sitting my little cousins, I was always around children. Ms. Chelsea was born Sept. 15, 1996. I had the pleasure of helping raise her alongside my husband, her father. Being a step-parent was unknown territory for me but I was excited to try. The fear of this unfamiliar transition caught me unprepared. How does one prepare for step-parenting and how do you know what to expect? You must go into parenting with a positive mind and a pure heart to love unconditionally, to make the best out of the situation. In July 1999, the excitement changed to fear when I found out I was expecting our first child. The fear of now having the responsibility of carrying a baby arose in me. The idea of being responsible for a baby residing

---

[31] Psalm 127:4 King James Version

inside me was scary. I had to prepare to be accountable for another life, to care, raise and be a good example for her. It changed my entire outlook on life. It was now more than playing peek-a-boo, and sending them on their way with their parents.

On April 21, 2000 Ms. Le'Kayla Nikole made her grand entrance into our lives. I was so unprepared as many first time moms are, but I was graced to be her mother. It is true, God's grace is sufficient[32] because shortly after Dec. 30, 2001 Ms. Le'Tavia Janiece was born. With this birth, we could not have fear, but just God. Le'Tavia was diagnosed with asthma at 8 months and she required our attention and care around the clock. She had to receive breathing treatments every four hours.

I am so thankful to God that He spoke to me the day before her first birthday and said, "Call the prayer warriors to pray for her at the exact time she was born and I will heal her." I

---

[32] II Corinthians 12:9 New International Version *But he said to me, "My grace is sufficient for you, for my power is made perfect in weakness." Therefore I will boast all the more gladly about my weaknesses, so that Christ's power may rest on me.*

was obedient and called on some people as we prayed for her, I went home bold in my faith and took her off all meds and she's 12 years old today and has not been dependent upon that machine since. I can never thank God enough for His blessing. His grace continued, we were blessed with an active baby girl Ms. LeKendra Leigh. She came into our lives and set order claiming her spot as the baby and daddy's little girl.

Prayer for Families

All wise and all-knowing God, it is because of you that we have the opportunity to become spouses and parents. Thank you for choosing us. I realize that we could not have done this without You. God I pray that as we enter this union of marriage that You will always be at the forefront of our relationship, of our marriage, and of our lives. God I ask, that You will be the foundation of our marriage and that everything that we establish together will be built on You. I thank You God for the gift of becoming parents to the precious children that you have given us. Even those that we did not physically birth, that we have obligation to lead and guide. Give us wisdom, give us the right words to say and the insight on how to be the parents and raise God-fearing children. We pray for covering over every family. God protect us and keep us as we live for you as a family, as one unit, worshipping You together, glorifying You together. We will always give You the praise. In Jesus Name! Amen!

Rejecting Fear and Reactivating Faith

"Now faith is the substance of things hoped for

the evidence of things not seen."

Hebrews 11:1 [33]

There comes a time in your life when you have to make mature decisions based on the fact that you deserve to live the best life God intends for you. There was a certain period in my life where I had to reject fear and reactivate my faith. I kept coming up short in many areas. Short in ministry, dead end corporate jobs, and in my gifting. I would always start-off full steam ahead with a great plan and good intentions. Somewhere, in the scheme of things, I would lose focus and the fear of 'what next?' convinced me to quit. Why would not knowing the next

---

[33] Hebrews 11:1 King James Version

level cause anyone to quit? It is uncomfortable being in a place where there is no clarity; so, to avoid the unknown, quitting seems practical and comforting.

Sometimes the fault lied in living my life for others. I did what people expected of me instead of doing what God told me to do. Being a P.K.[34] had its issues. We, my siblings and I, were often set on a pedestal because of our parents. Be we knew to be careful of man-made pedestals, because while the view is sweet, if people placed you there, they also believe they can take you down. Let God elevate, promote, and you will never fail.

At some point I realized, I could be more successful and further along in life, if I remained on task. The blessings that God had placed my name on were right in front of me. However, I detoured around them for what I thought made me feel secure.

---

[34] Preacher's/Pastor's Kid

I have not successfully maintained a corporate position. It is not because I am not a hard worker, I am. I have worked since my parents were able to stand me on a crate to look over the counter to take orders for the family printing company. I have always had visions and dreams of being my own boss and owing my own businesses. Nevertheless, every time I thought it did not look as if the business would be self-sustaining, I would stop working the vision, and return to corporate America. Not once did I consult God or allow Him room to sustain me through the rough patches. I started this cycle of accepting the first job that came along, hating it, and becoming so uncomfortable that I would leave. After years of this pattern, I made up my mind that it was time to finally reject fear.

Sometimes, God calls us to make unpopular decisions, ones that may not make sense to others. The purpose is so that he can get full glory from your obedience and thereby, shift you into your purpose. We each are unique, designed by God. I have accomplished some things that most of my peers have only dreamed. At 19, I married the man of my dreams and God maintains our love and union still, today. I am the proud mother of four ravishing young ladies, Chelsea, Le'Kayla, Le'Tavia, and Le'Kendra Hill. I actively serve my husband, my pastor in ministry at the Purposed Christian Church[35] where I hold the title of Executive Pastor. I am the CEO of Wounded Women Ministry, owner of Le'Ya's Boutique[36] and finally an author. Coming soon, I will be a solo recording artist, look out for Trish Hill.

I share this not to boast in my accomplishments because God gets all of the glory for all that he has done in and through me. I can do nothing without God. However, coming to this place of confidence is a direct result of letting go of the bondage that fear had on me. I am free now; free to allow God's

---

[35] Purposed Christian Church · 4416 West Gladys Ave. · Chicago, Illinois 60624
[36] Le'Ya's Boutique website · http//leya.storenvy.com

perfected plan dominate my life. For his divine purpose to consume my every day is breath to me.

I know some have endured far more than I have and survive to tell the story. We all have our journey and our paths vary from person to person. There is comfort in knowing, as we journey through life, that God is perfecting us for His glory. My Pastor[37] always says, "No Stress, No Strain, and No Struggle." These words have enlightened me and I will carry them in my spirit for the rest of my life.[38] No matter what we come against, God has the authority to get us through it.

Fear can paralyze, confuse, and cause you to become hopeless. However, as long as God is on your side, He can make any circumstance hopeful. The good thing about God is that he specializes in the impossible.[39] It is never too late to call on Him. When we cannot figure life out, God will work it out! From my

---

[37] Pastor LeAundre Hill, Pastor of Purposed Christian Church
[38] Pastor Hill, Thank you! I will always hold on to this nugget of wisdom!
[39] Luke 1:37 King James Version *For with God nothing shall be impossible.*

71

healthiest to my lowest depressed day, when I felt alone and unloved, God was there. However, He will not force Himself on you. He will wait with outstretched arms for your return. When you serve and have faith in God, it overrides anything that is standing against you.

Some of us are like a sad child, waiting on the response of a parent that is absent from sight. Waiting for what seems to be hours for an answer that is slow in coming. Most impatient children in this situation, scream out to the parent, rushing from room to room only to discover the parent was always close by. God is saying in this season, I am closer than you think. I am waiting on you to seek after me. Matthew 7:7[40] declares, "*Ask and it shall be given you, seek and ye shall find, knock and it shall be opened unto you*". Start to seek and He will be there.

---

[40] Matthew 7:7 King James Version

Prayer of Faith

Dear God of faith and wisdom, I pray that you will accept our endless desire to please You. As we have rejected fear, strain, struggle, and stress, I ask You heavenly Father, to fill us up with Your presence. God, I pray, as we reactivate our faith in You, it will be fresh and unwavering, so in the time of trouble we will be able to withstand the storm with You. God cover us as we let go of everything that we feel we need to survive this life. God, give us strength as we walk away from the normal order to do Your will. Guard our ear and eye gates from the distractions that may come against us to discourage us from doing what You have commanded for us to do. God, give us peace in knowing that everything will be well. I pray that our minds will be on You, and that we will not second-guess your plan but be steadfast in our calling. I pray for provision for the vision, oh God. Give us grace that will carry us to the next level in You. We declare that all we need is You oh God, nothing but You. I declare I have faith that you will see us through our new journey

in you. In Jesus' Name! Amen!

No Fear, Just God!

Fear of Letting Go

"Ye shall walk after the Lord *your God fear him, and keep his commandments and obey his voice, and ye shall serve him and cleave unto him."*

Deuteronomy 13:4[41]

It is human nature to hold things moot that may or may not be good for us. There are times we do not release things because we fear the unknown. What will happen to me if I let this steady *it* go? How will I live without *it*? How can I survive without *it*? If I leave *it*, I will have to start all over. These questions and statements plague the mind. The common thread that stitches these ponderings together is fear. We fear: the

---

[41] Deuteronomy 13:4 King James Version

unknown, being out of control in an area, leaving our comfort and many varying possibilities.

My life was filled with these episodes. The most frequent is letting go of toxic people in my life that I knew was a hazard to my health and spiritual growth. Letting go was not easy for me because I love completely and give 100%. I was always the one that wanted to make everyone better even if they did not appreciate me enough to give the same in return. There were people who attached themselves to me, not for me alone, but for the anointing that God placed on me. These people drained the life out of me, but I could not say no because I could not imagine not being in a position to help. The fear of moving forward without them created in my mind a void that would not go away. However, when I let them and *it* go, God filled the void immediately. When I weaned myself off those prescription drugs, God gave me sweet rest and I have never slept better.

When God has shifted and dealt with you, expect people to fall away. You will learn that some would rather deal with the crazy and unstable you in oppose to the saved and stable you. Friendships can be tested just by fully committing to God. Most leave because they fear being held accountable to the new standard that you have accepted. We are content in ignorance of doing better, but the moment values are raised; we are held accountable and should behave accordingly.

I charge and challenge every reader of this book to take self-inventory. Are there some things or someone that when you think of walking away, uncertainty and uneasy feelings appear? You know the circumstance may not be the best, yet you remain. This is what you need to let go. The stress and unhealthiness that comes along with certain relationships do nothing but stunt your growth. Opportunities dissipate because we are distracted by our *it*. No more waiting for confirmations, if you want to save your life, it is time to let your *it* go.

Prayer of Letting Go

Father God in Heaven,

Thank You for always being a God that gives us the things and the people we need to live healthy and purposeful lives in You. God I ask that you forgive us for not trusting you. God forgive us for not allowing You full access to take over our situations. Forgive us God of not letting go when you told us to. Holding on to things that was not Your will for our lives, please forgive us. Create in us oh God a clean heart and renew the right spirit within us. As we find the courage to let go, God be with us. As we pack up our things and walk away God, be with us, as we hand in two week notices to jobs that are not lined up with our destiny, God be with us. I trust You oh God! As we let go of fear that has controlled our thinking, that has controlled our outlook, God be with us. I know that fear is not of You, so I release it and let it GO! Every void we face God, please fill it

79

with Your grace, fill it with Your peace. I can never get enough

of You. It is in Your Son Jesus' name, I pray, Amen.

No Fear, Just God!

Just God

"For God so loved the World

that he gave his only begotten Son,

that whosoever believeth in him should not perish

but have everlasting life.

For God sent not his Son to condemn the world,

but through him might be saved."

John 3: 16-17[42]

The ultimate desire of God for us is that we abandon fear

and live freely through Him; no restrictions and no restraints,

only God. When all is said and done, the effort it takes to be free

is done in vain if we are not living a saved life. It makes no

sense to go through the motions of wanting and needing God

when, in the end, we reject His salvation for our lives.

---

[42] John 3:16-17 King James Version

Sometimes, I imagine a summer breeze, floating on soft clouds, sun beaming on my face and not even questioning who is carrying me, because I trust the hand that is holding me.

God is a God of faith. He finds pleasure in loving and caring for His own. Therefore, we should have no reason to doubt his love or his care for us. God is all purity, no preservatives added. He is God and God alone. He requires no help. He rules and reigns above any and everything. Nothing compares to Him. Ultimately, He is all that we have.

I have experienced hurt in many places, even in the church. It was to the extent that I felt I had no place of refuge. There was no peace. However, when I was down to nothing, God was there to pick me up and give me life.

Upon reading this chapter, I pray that you feel compelled to accept God as your salvation if you do not a solid relationship with Him. He has not forgotten about you and desires to help you. Once I focused on Him, my days of living in fear are behind me. My walk with God is stronger and better than before.

If you do not take away anything else, please know, with God, all things, every dream, vision, thought, is possible as long as you have faith in Him. My life has changed and has never been the same since I made God my choice.

The only time fear is acceptable for a believer, is when we actively fear God. He is the only one to fear. To fear God is let go of our personal agendas, connect to His righteous standards, and do all to honor Him. David, a man after the very heart of God, asked in Psalm 86:11[43], *Teach me thy way, O Lord; I will walk in thy truth: unite my heart to fear thy name.* He does not want us to fear Him as we would something that frightens us. He desires reverence and ultimate respect that comes with not allowing ourselves to risk being anything other than upright in His eyes.

---

[43] Psalm 86:11 King James Version

There are many promises associated with the fear of God. They include but are not limited to these: wisdom[44], faithful provision[45], mercy[46], and holiness[47]. How can we not reverence a God that keeps His word to us! Numbers 23:19[48] states: *God is not a man, that he should lie; neither the son of man, that he should repent: hath he said, and shall he not do it? or hath he spoken, and shall he not make it good?* His word will not return to Him void.[49].

The way we can live a fear free life is by accepting Jesus into our hearts. God sent His son to die on the cross to save us. God made a fearless decision to sacrifice his only son for you,

---

[44] Proverbs 9:10 King James Version *The fear of the LORD is the beginning of wisdom: and the knowledge of the holy is understanding.*

[45] Psalm 34:9 King James Version *O fear the LORD, ye his saints: for there is no want to them that fear him.*

[46] Psalm 103:11 King James Version *For as the heaven is high above the earth, so great is his mercy toward them that fear him.*

[47] II Corinthians 7:1 King James Version *Having therefore these promises, dearly beloved, let us cleanse ourselves from all filthiness of the flesh and spirit, perfecting holiness in the fear of God.*

[48] Numbers 23:19 King James Version

[49] Isaiah 55:11 King James Version *So shall my word be that goeth forth out of my mouth: it shall not return unto me void, but it shall accomplish that which I please, and it shall prosper in the thing whereto I sent it.*

so that you can live in this sin filled world, without the worry of anything.

One of my favorite songs has always been, *"It is Well with My Soul"*. It took me going through some things to realize that God has it all under control. Even when I tried to handle situations I felt capable of handling, I found I could not do it alone. I still had to call on God. There is a line in the song that says, "whatever my lot, thou has taught me to say, it is well with my soul." No matter what we go through, it can be well with our souls. We trust that God is going to keep His promises to us.

Remember just as easy as we accept fear into our lives know that it can take precedence over our belief and trust in God. Do not let fear separate you from the most important relationship you could ever have. Whatever it is, God specializes in the impossible and unthinkable. Nothing, absolutely nothing is too hard for my God. You are G.L.A.M.[50]

Every shortcoming, every imperfection, God loves all of you.

---

[50] G.L.A.M. God Loves All of Me. An annual conference provided and sponsored by Prophetess PaTricia Hill and Purpose Christian Church

Prayer Just With God

Father God in Heaven,

An all-knowing God, whom we serve and depend on. It is my prayer that the person reading this book will make a decision to make You their choice. I pray for a quickening in their spirit that will spark their soul to be drawn to You. It is my desire that more people see you God, and make a choice to get rid of fear and things that hinder them from being close to You. Oh God, let them feel Your presence and hold them so close Your sweet fragrance will fill their nostrils. We need Your direction and we need to hear Your voice. Lord of all, rule our lives, and speak to us now. I pray that my brothers and sisters accept You today, that they will follow You all the days of their life. There will be no doubt or concern with who You are. Lighten their load, I pray that they lay their burdens down at your feet and never pick them back up again. God, allow them to see You and Your mighty works. Most of all, God let them see You in me. I pray that through this journey someone was able to receive You for themselves.

I pray that through my obedience in releasing NO Fear, Just God, someone's life has been changed and impacted for the better. I am in awe of Your glory oh God, and how you took me and gave me the assignment. God I am so grateful for being put in the position to help guide and lead Your people closer to You. Thank You for always giving me a great ending in You. I will forever give You all the Praise. I will forever bless Your name of God, for Your loving kindness toward me. Thank you God for sending every person that was key in helping me complete this accomplishment, those that pushed, prayed and encouraged me. God, I owe you my life, and I will serve you for the rest of my days. In Jesus Name! Amen!

No Fear, Just God

When Fear Happens

It's like you're stuck on a ship without a Captain

It started off as a smooth ride

But somewhere fear came in like a violent tide

Shaking and moving out of control

This thing called Fear was truly on a roll

But that's not how God intended for this to be

Because he has not given us the spirit of fear you see

My mind is supposed to be sound and full of love

When I reflect on Him it carries me up like a dove

In our mind is where we create this emotion

We attach ourselves and use it like a love potion

But it don't help us, it hurt us

And when you think about how fear tricked you,

it makes you wanna cuss

91

But you refrain

Because you remember a name

And name that's above all others

The moment you realize that God has always had your back

And he has the power to cover all lack

No Stress, No Struggle, No Strain

Fears job is to come and leave a stain

Stain all your hopes and dreams

But that all can change when you switch teams

Team fear is not the winning squad

You have automatic victory, with Team God

No Fear Just God

It's not hard

It's simply rejecting Fear and Reactivating Faith

Accepting His plan and Will

He can make all things possible if you just keep still

No Longer Fear, Just God

Steps in Overcoming Your Fears

- Recognize and acknowledge what the fear is
- Find the root of the fear (when did it start, how did it start,)
- Uproot it (prayer, fasting, rebuking it before it takes root, calling it by name)
- Add it to your daily prayer (pray against it every day, until you feel a release from the strong hold)
- Give God Glory for your victory over Fear (Giving God Glory will in turn give you the strength and courage to stand against fear)
- Share with others (your testimony will impact the lives of others that struggle with the same fear)

No Fear, Just God!

Acknowledgements

Wonderful Husband

A special thank you goes to my loving husband of 15 years, Pastor LeAundre Hill. You have always pushed me out of my comfort zone to pursue my Purpose. Babe, I love you so much and I appreciate you for everything that you do.

Thank You to My Kids

Chelsea, Le'Kayla, Le'Tavia, and Le'Kendra. Thanks for supporting Mommy and being my biggest cheerleaders. Always remember Christian Pretty Girls Rock!

My Handsome God Boys

Christian Kevon, Marreon De'Mari, and Jordyn Isaiah
Every time I see you, my room lights up... I thank God for the three of you.

Parents' Praise

I have the best Parents in the world! You have taught and given me so much in life. I am who I am because of you and I hope that I'm making you proud.
Thanks for your support throughout the years.

Pastor Norman and Diane Donahue Sr.
Melba Hill – Rowry

Glorious God-Parents

Thank You for accepting the awesome task of joining my
parents in covering me in love and prayer.
Late Chester and Charlene Scott
Late Benjamin Donahue
Late Alva Carne
Pastor Kenneth and Veneeta Phelps

Sibling Smiles

Tavia - My best buddy, my shopping partner, you're simply the
greatest big sister a girl could ever ask for. Thank you for your
guidance and your love for me.
June and Kevin – My big brothers who have always protected
me and kept me covered. You two are amazing and I would go
to the end of the earth and back for you.
Cynthia and Tatianna – Hey you two thanks for being awesome
sister in laws, you girls hold a special place in my heart.
Lonale Rowry – My baby brother that I love to pieces.
Kanisha Rowry – Your quiet demeanor has no measurement to
the big heart that you have for people. That's what I admire
about you the most.

Circle of Friends

I have a close circle that I keep around me that has been very
influential in this process and I want you to know that I could
not have done this without you… I know if I begin to name
people I may miss someone, but you certainly know who you
are (M.S., J.T., D.R., E.L.,Y.B., T.D., L.H.*2, K.L,
C.G.,L.J.,S.O.)

Family

To my family Donahue's, Bostics, Whites, Bonds, Scotts,
Scarboroughs, Hills, Bibbs
Deacon Maurice and Brenda Donahue
Deacon Fernando Donahue
Deacon James Dixon
Arlene Donahue
Claudia Bostic
Carl Bostic
Ronald and Hattie Burns
Evangelist Gwenette Burns

Special...Special Thanks to my covenant Pastors, Brothers and Sisters

Pastor Reggie and London Royal
Pastor Antoine and La'Kisha Sanders
Pastor Vidal and Lisa Cargo
Pastor David and Tamera Pope
Pastor Christopher and Brittany Swims
Pastor Leverette and Jeton Bryant
Pastor Bobby and Sabrina Strickland
Pastor Tim and Kelli Howard

So Much To My Editing Team!
Yolanda Simmons-Battle "Dr. Yo"
Cheryl Shumake
Shawna-Joy Ogunleye

And To the Best Church in the Whole Wide World

The Purposed Church
I love each and every one of you.... Romans 8:28

About the Author

Prophetess PaTricia Ann Donahue-Hill was born in Maywood, IL. December 13, 1979, as the youngest child to Pastor Norman and Lady Dianne Donahue. Being a sick baby, the doctors had given up on her but her praying parents did not give up on God. God manifested a miracle. PaTricia grew to become a healthy and blessed child. She graduated from St. Eulalia Elementary school, 94 and Proviso East High School 98. With a passion for cosmetology, she continued on to Pivot Point International School of Design, 99, becoming a licensed Cosmetologist. Immediately after graduation on May 2, 1999, PaTricia married the love of her life, Rev. LeAundre D. Hill. God blessed her with one of the greatest gifts of a women and that is to birth three beautiful daughters into the world, Le'Kayla, Le'Tavia, and Le'Kendra and a wedding gift Chelsea.

Growing up a preacher's daughter, PaTricia was raised in the church and at an early age took on the passion for music at the Mt. Hebron Baptist Church singing in the choir. She continued with that passion as her father Pastor Norman Donahue Sr. was led by God to organize Three Crosses of Calvary M.B. Church. PaTricia has sung recorded and shared the stage over the years in the gospel industry with New Direction, Gray Boy Productions, JC Ensemble, Bethel Green Family Worship Center Choir, Marlowe Cribbs and Friends and many others.

Although she loves singing, Patricia surrendered to the will and call of God to preach the Gospel and minister to God's people not only through song but also through God's Word. On Sunday October 7, 2007, she preached her first sermon before the body of Christ at Three Crosses of Calvary Church. It is there where Evangelist Hill has served as an Associate Minister and Minister of Music.

In February 2012, Pastor and Lady Hill re-launched the Purposed Church, where she serves as the Executive Pastor and a Praise Team Singer. Prophetess Hill also is the founder of Wounded Women Ministry, a ministry that was birthed to aid and uplift women from all walks of life. No matter the race, or religion the assignment is to serve and assist with whatever resources or tools possible to help motivate them to live the best life that God has intended for us to live.

June 9, 2013 Evangelist PaTricia Hill was licensed and ordained as Prophetess Patricia Hill.

No Fear, Just God!

References

Bible Gateway, a division of the Zondervan Corporation, 3900

Sparks Drive SE, Grand Rapids, MI 49546 USA

Effective Mind Control

http://www.effective-mind-control.com/about-this-website.html

Webster Dictionary

http://www.merriam-webster.com